THE
WATERHOLE
MILLIONAIRE

THE WATERHOLE MILLIONAIRE

PRINCIPLES FROM A VILLAGE WARRIOR THAT WILL TURNAROUND YOUR FINANCIAL LIFE

S. Gabriel Shumba

munaii

USA, England, South Africa

The Waterhole Millionaire, Copyright © 2014 by S. Gabriel Shumba

S. Gabriel Shumba/Munaii Bookworks
6565 N. MacArthur Blvd.
Irving, TX 75039
www.munaii.com

Publisher's Note: This is a work of fiction. Names, characters, places, and incidents are a product of the author's imagination. Locales and public names are sometimes used for atmospheric purposes. Any resemblance to actual people, living or dead, or to businesses, companies, events, institutions, or locales is completely coincidental.

Book Layout ©2014 Munaii Bookworks

Ordering Information:
Quantity sales - Special discounts are available on quantity purchases by schools, corporations, associations, and others. For details, contact the "Special Sales Department" at the address above.

The Waterhole Millionaire/ S. Gabriel Shumba -- 1st ed.
ISBN 978-0-9861018-1-6

*To **my late mother**, Christine Jessica Munyaka, every word you spoke into my life, is being revealed in my strength to endure the tests of life. Thank you very much.*

*To **my wife**, Miriam, thank you for being my inspiration and guide. I love you dearly.*

*To **my son Washe**, for whom I also wrote this book; read it over and over until you positively impact millions of lives. I am very proud of you.*

*To **my support team**, I am ever so thankful for the roles each of you assumed. The journey has been long, and I thank you for your presence in my life. I am super grateful.*

The more important people are to you, the more important money will be to you.

—Dr. Mike Murdock

To change your life permanently,
you must change another life profoundly.

—S. Gabriel Shumba

Contents

Introduction

The law of first things states that if you get the *first thing* right, the next falls into place. And yet life is full of people that are yet to find their *first thing* – that one thing that will create a domino effect of successful results meant to change their lives forever. Perhaps you are like many others who have struggled to find their *first thing*. If you are, then this book is it, your *first thing*. This book narrates a set of principles that will trigger a series of results meant to make you the next *Waterhole Millionaire*. The term millionaire as applied in this book is not about teaching you to make a million dollars; it is about helping you define financial independence at any income level. The subject of success while not mastered by the majority has long been figured out by many people. What is known is that success is not aligned to race, geography, background or education; it simply follows focus and committed action. Once you discover these principles, once you learn them, and practice them; they will transform the ordinary you, into the extraordinary you in a short space of time, that might frighten you.

Why do I state all this? What gives me the right or the ability to make such distinct and evident statements? I want to confess right off the bat that I actually wrote this book for me. My life has been full of meandering challenges, successes and downright mediocrity. After graduating from college, I promised my mother that I would be a millionaire within the following ten years. At the time, I enjoyed all the potential any young man could possess; the education, the career and the hunger for success. Although I had come close many times, my mother died before I became a millionaire. It felt as if she had been waiting for me to fulfill my promise.

I began to write this book as a manual to help me turn my life around, and indeed my life slowly began to change. It started with a change in my perspective, and was followed by a change in the things I regarded as important. Then came a change in my method of getting things done. Big business opportunities started to open up as I slowly progressed in living my writing. I gave the book to some of my friends and family members and became astounded by how a few principles I had laid out for myself had moved them with equal intensity. Some of them began to show me lists of things they had learned from my manual. One day I had a discussion with a close friend, and he told me not to add my lessons at the end of the book because each reader was going to learn something different from reading it. I agreed, so I took out all the lessons I learned from the experience, except for one.

The most important lesson I learned in my life changing process was that money follows personal improvement. That means it follows results of positive shifts in a person's life, business and community. I finally got it: Whenever I contributed to the transformation of somebody's life for better, I attracted favor, and whenever I attracted favor, money became easy to make; whenever I made money, I found more opportunities to change more lives, and so began to attract even more favor and more money, so the cycle continued. This process is what I refer to as *lasting impact*. Impact can be defined as having a strong and lasting effect on one's life or on the lives of others. In order to make that level of impact possible, money has to be a key part of the equation, and here is why. There are 24 hours in a day, and after removing time for healthy sleep, that leaves 16 available potentially productive hours on a daily basis. On average 75% of those available hours (*12 hours*) are spent on income generating activities such as work, commute, networking, preparation and learning. This means that an average adult wakes up with an income goal, and as a result, goes on to commit the majority of their day towards income generating activities. So it goes without saying that money dominates the lives of most people around you because they all live in a global system that demands currency as a primary representation of value.

So let me ask you a quick question; whose life have you changed in the past five years? You could be missing an opportunity of a lifetime because the more important people are to you, the more important money will become to you. And to get the money, you must begin to produce definitive results in your personal life, business or community. So this book outlines the foundational principles necessary to create radical change in your life, your business or your community. It is about generating a series of results that enable you to accumulate enough financial resources to redefine your own life and subsequently use those resources to impact other people's lives in a profound way. Age, status, geography, gender, language, race and education are not credible obstacles in your pursuit of a better life, business or community. You have absolutely no excuse for failing to become a *Waterhole Millionaire* – a person who becomes financially independent by solving a pervasive problem affecting their life, and then helping others to do the same.

For a dream comes through much activity.
—Ecclesiastes 5:3

CHAPTER ONE

FACE THE LION WHEN IT ATTACKS

It was early summer in the village of Zimuto, when Chief Gato gathered his high council to discuss the crop challenges of the season. As was always the case, Chief Gato opened the midday session with a prayer and was about to get into his welcome speech when he was interrupted by two ladies wrapped in colorful linen and carrying woven baskets on top of their heads.

"Come, my children, put the tea over there, by that gentleman," the Chief said while stepping into the shade of a Msasa tree, and the ladies obliged.

Moments later, the council of 15 men of high position in their respective surrounding communities, were sipping the hot Tanganda tea – a blend of tea grown in the eastern highlands of Zimbabwe. In a joyous mood, Chief Gato opened his long-awaited speech:

"Let me welcome you to my home, men of Zimuto. As you know, the purpose of this meeting is to discuss food-sharing in case the rains continue to fuss at our land. I want last season's storage to be released in seven weeks if the rains don't fall before then."

All eyes were on the chief, a large-framed man who was slightly overweight. His round face complemented his broad smile and his deep voice commanded respect. Chief Gato had been chief of Zimuto since the death of his father ten years earlier. All men of Zimuto respected his well-balanced intelligence and influence over a broad complement of the Zimuto population. As he continued with his speech, unexpectedly a distant sound became audible to the ears of council members. The chief stopped mid-sentence to pay attention to the sound of a horn coming from a distance. Cow horns were sounded in cases of emergency; in reaction, the men of the council stood and stared in the direction of the horning sound. Two village warriors began to trot towards the direction of the sound, in order to meet with the messenger, as was the practice in the village.

A tall, slim, and shabbily dressed man appeared out of breath as the two warriors held each of his arms to support his light frame in their approach.

"Water! Give him water, now," the Chief ordered.

After taking a few quick sips, the man introduced himself.

"I am Miso, son of Gonde, and have travelled from the hunting grounds to bring you sad news. Sani, our most talented hunter, was attacked by a lion near the top of the mountain."

The chief was tongue-tied for a moment before he hand-signaled the messenger to continue with the message.

"The village healers have been called. Sani was alive when I left with the message."

"Which mountain?" one of the councilmen asked.

"Gutu, Mount Gutu!" the messenger exclaimed after taking another sip from the cup of water he was holding in his right hand.

With urgency, the chief summoned his cattle-drawn cart to be brought. Within half an hour, the chief, the messenger and two advisors to the chief were riding in a cart ahead of another carrying five village warriors on their way to the scene of the attack. It was clear that the chief was visibly shaken because it was certainly not the news he was expecting on the day he was to introduce his best village collaboration plan yet. What made it worse was the fact that he had personally asked Sani to accompany a team of less-experienced hunters in order to increase the chances of bringing food home. Sani had become somewhat disinterested in the hunting trade despite holding the village record for bringing the most beasts home from a hunt. Chief and Sani grew up together and were best friends;

they even married sisters. Sani always boasted about marrying the better-looking sister – behind the chief's back, of course. Sani was a product of Gato senior's warrior-training program. The chief's father was very fond of Sani and often referred to him as one of his sons. So what exactly had happened?

As the two carts left the compound, the messenger began to explain in more detail the events that led to the attack.

"Ironically, the event began when news from a local shepherd reached our group of hunters that a pride of lions had been sighted tracking livestock in the southern forests. As a result, Sani ordered us out of the forests to head towards the mountains. He explained to the group, the theory that lions seldom hunt in the mountain because they are lazy creatures. They prefer an easy catch, so they hunt in forests and valleys."

"He was right." The Chief agreed with the statement.

The messenger paused to confirm that the Chief was done responding, "So we hiked for one hour to reach the edge of the mountain. We made our way up Mount Gutu; it was not long before we discovered a herd of antelope feasting on umbrella bushes. Using hand gestures, Sani signaled for the "cow-horn" formation, sending members of our team scattering in a semi-circle fashion while he remained in the middle. Sani loves this battle formation that I heard was popularized by Shaka, the Zulu warrior, during his reign in the Eastern Cape region of South Africa. It was being applied in that instance to surprise the herbivores and trap them inside the hunters' semi-circle."

The messenger paused for a few seconds before he proceeded to narrate the details of the attack.

"I was positioned to Sani's left and I thought I had a much better view of events than him. I should have shouted when I saw the big cat charge towards him. I was sure it was going after the antelope bull directly in front of Sani."

The messenger's eyes became watery as he began to narrate the most difficult part of Sani's ordeal.

"What happened next caused a scene I have never witnessed during game hunting throughout my life in Zimuto. A big lion, with reddish-black mane, sprung from a nearby bush and charged in the direction of Sani; upon seeing the danger, Sani stood still with his spear raised, facing the oncoming lion. However, before he could release the spear, the lion struck him on the chest using its right forelimb. By the time Sani hit the ground, the other members of the group were already running ahead of the herd. It was a comical scene to see a herd of antelopes chasing twelve spear-wielding grown men down the mountain. As I stood in shock, one of the warriors nearest to Sani also witnessed every detail of the attack as it unfolded. In panic and reflex, the warrior threw his spear but missed the lion completely; however, it appeared as though the maneuver caused the lion to flee. As the lion struggled to get over a rock, I noticed that Sani's spear was dug into the side of the lion, penetrating its body from below the belly. I later learned from the other warrior that before the Lion struck him, Sani had managed to push his spear in to its belly. After regaining my energy, I walked towards Sani and found him lying on his back in the brown soil, groaning from the immense pain through his upper body and on his left arm.

The other warrior who had braved the chase to witness the attack came to help me pick Sani up and carry him down the mountain."

"Clever men! Lions do not hunt alone. If Sani had been left lying there, other lions would have come to finish the job," the chief remarked, while his advisors nodded in agreement.

"After a while, a few of the men came to help us carry the wounded body of Sani. Before we realized it, we had reached a stream located about half a mile from the mountain. We began to use water to clean his wounds while others gave instructions for the village healers to be called and the chief to be informed."

"Where did you leave him?"

"I left him lying near the stream still groaning from his chest and back wounds, Chief," the messenger phrased the urgency of his message in a high-pitched voice.

Before dusk, the chief and his cart had reached the river-bank and knew exactly where to go because they had sight of a group of people surrounding Sani. The village healers were already there, and a prayer team had been summoned to inter-cede on behalf of Sani. The healers had disinfected and cleaned Sani's wounds with herbal medicines; they had also given him some flower roots to chew in order to chill the pain.

"Masikati Chief?" the lead healer greeted the Chief.

"Afternoon to you too," the chief responded. "How is our injured doing?"

"He is in pain but he will be alright because the jaws of the lion did not take his hand. He fought hard, Chief; he really never gave up the fight despite being under vicious attack. The claws caught his chest and back but did not touch any vital organs."

"I am relieved. Thank you for your good work."

"He is our son, Chief. It is an honor to help."

The chief ordered for Sani to be put in his cart and told everybody to leave for their homes before it became dark.

"Listen everyone, lions love to hunt in the dark and they have already smelled human blood. Please, leave for your homes immediately and secure your livestock. I will accompany Sani to his home, where I will spend the night."

It was not long before the crowd dispersed and the chief was sitting in his ox-drawn cart on his way to Sani's home. A message had been sent ahead to Tariro, Sani's wife, commonly referred to as Mai Tee (Tee's mother). Tariro and Sani's first son was called Tindo, shortened to "Tee" by village citizens.

"I always thought I would die before you do," the chief said, looking into the eyes of Sani. "I am overweight and always stressed by village matters. But here we are, you decide to go in a heroic fashion – you never cease to amaze me, my friend."

Sani was silent, an unusual occurrence because he always responded to the chief's verbal jabs. That silence sent shockwaves around the chief's body. His interpretation of it was that Sani was seriously injured and beyond recovery, otherwise he would have responded. So the chief kept quiet and for another half an hour nobody spoke until Sani stretched his uninjured hand and smiled at the chief.

"I have to tell you something very important in case I don't make it," Sani whispered to the chief.

"Don't speak like that, Baba Tee," the chief politely reprimanded his friend.

"No, let me say what I have to say in front of these witnesses," Sani continued. "I always wanted to tell you th... ahhhh!" Sani groaned with pain.

"Stop talking and rest," the chief pleaded with him.

"Let him talk, it may be important, Chief. He seems to be in a lot of pain, so let the man speak in case his family needs to know what he has to say," one of the chief's advisors requested.

So Sani continued, "Chief, I have always wanted to let you know that I married the more beautiful sister."

The whole cart broke out in laughter. They laughed so loud that the people in the cart following behind them were puzzled by the joyous noise.

"You are still your old self, Sani of Zimuto," the chief happily proclaimed.

"The hunting grounds choose their own events, Chief. All we can do is decide how to respond to such events." Sani finally exchanged thoughts with his best friend, the Chief of Zimuto.

"Yes, yes..." Chief Gato agreed with Sani.

"I can choose to die from this or live. I choose to live and fight, my friend. This will not be the picture of how I have lived life; it cannot end like this, not this way. It is the beginning of my purpose." Sani paused, and then continued. "Wipe away any tears you may have – I will outlive every person inside this cart."

CHAPTER TWO

PICK A VILLAGE PROBLEM TO SOLVE

The patient and the chief's delegation were now about a quarter of a mile away from Sani's compound. Sani's homestead was quiet and dark, as expected at that time of the day. As the cart approached, a black shadowy figure became more visible. The figure began to approach the cart slowly and, almost in a sudden change of mind, turned around and broke into a full sprint going back towards the compound.

"They are here! Baba is here!" Joni, a neighborhood teenager shouted to draw the attention of a group of people gathered around a campfire.

S. GABRIEL SHUMBA

Immediately, about twelve men stood up and began running towards the cart. They signaled the cart to move towards the center of the compound. Every person, except Sani, got out of the cart as the warriors circled it in preparation for new orders. The chief's eyes were now directed at an opening being created by the crowd to let a special woman through. Mai Tee approached and stood next to the cart. She was wrapped in black cloth and with a white bandana around her head. Her arms moved loudly because of heaped bangles occupying the lower ends of her arms. She wore colorful beads around her long neck, as was customary for all women of high standing in the community. Without dispute, she was the most beautiful woman most men had seen in the Zimuto area, and her slim figure seemed to disguise the fact that she was a mother of one son and three daughters. No wonder Sani was the proudest husband in the village.

The chief addressed Sani's wife. "Mai Tee, I am sorry for your pain."

She did not respond. However, her eyes acknowledged the chief as she turned to lean against the cart and look at her husband, who was still lying flat in the cart.

"You look handsome, Baba Tee," she said, looking into his eyes.

Sani just smiled and said, "I am fine, Mai Tee, the pain has subsided and I am happy to see you."

"Baba Tee, I should be happy to see you alive."

18

Mai Tee paused for a moment, examining her husband's wounds before Sani spoke.

"Get me out of here, please," Sani requested, looking at the chief.

The chief ordered the warriors to carry Sani into the hut directly before them. It served as a guest bedroom that one of the village healers had set up for Sani. After an hour of informal planning sessions, the chief and his crew took rest around the burning campfire; Mai Tee and her husband were inside the warm hut.

The next morning everybody was well rested. More and more guests kept coming in. From the northern community of Zimuto came seven representatives of families, three from the east and twenty from the southern side. The chief lived in the south of Zimuto where Sani's wife was born and raised. What surprised everybody was the presence of a large number of people who seldom visited Sani; they mostly knew him through third parties.

"Where do all these people know Sani from?" one gentleman asked.

"By word of mouth from neighbors and relatives," the chief responded. "Reputation is what people say about you, and character is who you are. When your good character matches your reputation, people become attracted to you."

It was not long before the two medical officers from the government's mobile clinic arrived. They spent most of the morning attending to Sani, using a weird-looking machine to take pictures and inject liquid into his body. Finally, they came out to report some news to the family and the village citizens, who were eager to hear the status of their beloved warrior.

"He will be fine, but will not be able to use his left arm for much more than supporting his right arm. We will train the village healers to administer pain medication and antibiotics. Other than that, he will be walking in two weeks."

Everyone was happy Sani was alive, but Mai Tee was overwhelmed with conflicting emotions. She was grateful her husband had survived, but very disturbed that he would not be able to use his left arm. Sani was left-handed, and as a hunter, his left hand was the source of income for the family. Even if he was to turn to agriculture, he would still need his left hand. Mai Tee's son, Tindo, embraced his mother with warm arms to keep her from crying further.

"It will be fine, Mother. Since when do we have to worry about anything in this family?"

At that moment, Mai Tee noticed that her tears had been witnessed by a few guests, so she immediately wiped them away using a loose part of her garment. Soon after, the government's medical officers departed, leaving a box full of medication for Sani. They promised to return in three weeks.

The government employed medical officers who were

trained nurses and doctors to travel around isolated villages and administer medical assistance as well as medical and hygiene education. They visited most villages twice every month using mobile clinic vehicles. They were also available in the event of an emergency, as was the case with Sani.

One Month Later...

Sani woke up in a rare, happy mood one morning. His wife mentioned to him that she had not seen the happy face he was wearing in almost a month. He turned to her and said, "Mai Tee, tell Tindo that I am having lunch with him in the main hut today; my plan for the future is now clear in my head. I am excited about what we are going to accomplish as a family."

"Baba Tee, what plan? Don't forget your arm cannot function as well as it did before. If you are going to tell me you are taking Tindo hunting, I will pour cold water on you," his wife warned him.

"Let me talk to my son alone, please. We have to find a way of feeding this family – after all, the strength of a fish is in the water. This is my water...."

She interrupted him; "Let younger hunters teach Tindo the new tricks – you cannot take him to the hunting grounds in your condition."

Sani cast a glance full of disappointment at his wife and left the room after grudgingly wishing her a good morning. He paced around the compound the entire morning, looking at the cattle kraal, the chicken pen and the vegetable garden that Mai Tee and his daughters had maintained over the years. As a very experienced hunter, Sani often caught four beasts every week; kept one to feed his family for the month and sold the rest to villagers in order to raise money for buying grain and other essentials.

Back in the hut, Mai Tee began to wonder whether her husband was about to take more risks by going hunting in his current condition, with his very young and inexperienced son. She had witnessed too many stories of attacks on humans by hyenas, lions and snakes and knew all too well that many hunters did not return home to their families over the years. To her, hunting in the Zimuto forests was like sending a husband or son to a battlefield: every moment they spent away felt like imprisonment. The helplessness and the worry were too unbearable.

Shortly after midday during the summer's week, Sani sat in the main hut facing his son to have lunch. Tindo had been informed by his mother that his father wanted to speak with him about a serious future matter. Any average person could tell that Tindo had been coached on how to respond to certain questions prior to the meeting. He had also been groomed on how to counter any point raised by Sani about going to the hunting grounds for training.

"Son, you are now eighteen, and as you know, I am injured and can no longer provide for the family the old way," he remarked as Tindo listened attentively. "You and I will have to start working together in order to provide for this family; you must leave school, Tindo."

"But why, father? I am in my last year of high school and have a few months left before I can to go to the city and attend university," Tindo said, trying to convince his dad to change his mind.

"Listen, son. We have a drought year; schools will close because of lack of water in a few weeks. If you do not eat, you cannot learn. This family does not have two years to wait for food. I need you to trust me and work with me to change the history of this family." Sani was looking right into his son's eyes. "

"What history?" Tindo asked.

"For as long as you've known life, this family has been living hand-to-mouth, working hard all day long to have just enough to eat, and nothing to give away. I am sick and tired of that lifestyle."

"Baba, how is my hunting going to change that scenario?"

"Don't put words in my mouth, son. I did not say you should

go hunting."

"Baba, my teacher told me that the future of any human being is built in education. Without it, we cannot continue to eat or have enough wealth to share."

"Your teacher is partially right. Education prepares you, but exposure is what changes you, Tindo."

Tindo could tell that his father's approach in the meeting had been well thought out, possibly for months, if not years.

"You see, whenever you are exposed to different events or experiences, you also learn from them, just like in school. The only risk is that if you are not learning from your mistakes, you will never get any further than you were at the moment of the mistake."

"Baba, sometimes it is not mistakes that prevent you from succeeding. Look at you, father, you did nothing wrong, but go hunting in the very way you knew how. But out of nowhere, a lion changed your destiny."

"The lion did not change my destiny. Only I have the ability to shape or change my own destiny. Unfortunate events have occurred and we all will encounter a fair share of them at some point in the future. However, it is not what happens that determines your future success, it is what you do after it happens that will shape the nature of your success."

Tindo remained silent as his father spoke the wisdom passed down to him by his own father and village elders; it was indeed a heartwarming experience shared between father and son. Such meetings were a rarity in the Zimuto culture. Fathers commonly communicated to their sons only in an instructive manner; they seldom listened to their children's perspectives in order to guide them better. For Tee to have such a candid discussion with his well-respected father was a breakthrough moment he had not previously experienced in his life.

"Father, as you know I had already started hunting lessons and I have had some success. I am ready to listen to what you have to say about hunting; I heard you – school may not be feasible right now, but I do see my next ability in hunting just like you."

"Tindo, hunting is what every young man in Zimuto is learning today. The forests are becoming smaller and the number of people is increasing every year. If I force you to go hunting today, we will all die of hunger in the next few years."

"But this is a drought year, and during drought everybody goes hunting because there are no rains for fields and gardens."

"Yes, son, you are right on point. However, I am not going to teach you how to jump into potential failure. I am here to help you jump into potential success. That is what my father taught me and I intend to pass it on to you."

"I can now see what made you a good hunter – you are very determined," Tindo said, complimenting his father.

"What made me a good hunter was that when everybody else was looking for grazers to hunt, I looked for greener bushes grazers enjoyed feeding on. I would wait there for hours and finally they would come to eat. From that point on, my problem was how many grazers to kill," Sani proudly explained as his son showed signs of acknowledgement on his face.

"My father taught me to look for a problem and not an opportunity. If you look for a problem and then go on to find a solution, then you are better off than someone who looks for an opportunity."

"What do you mean baba?"

"Son, an opportunity is a solution to a problem; that means someone else solved the problem and they are the one enjoying success. If you want great success, you must find a problem and create a solution for it – more like creating your own opportunity."

"I see."

"Drought is a problem affecting every village household this year, and while everybody is hunting, very few people are bringing beasts home. This is so because grazers can sense when drought is nearing and will begin to migrate. To survive or even excel, you must identify an idea that supports a serious village problem, and begin work on creating a satisfying solution."

"Do you mean a solution to prevent the drought?"

"If you can find one, I am sure it would qualify, but I am not talking about something that complex. Good ideas are usually very simple – they are easy to understand and execute."

"OK, tell me, baba, what do you want me to do? I am at your command."

"I thought you wouldn't ask. I have an idea that addresses a serious problem that grazers are experiencing. The solution to the grazers' problem will affect our family's future, possibly the future of the entire village, but as you can see, I cannot execute the solution myself. I need to know that you will walk with me and do what I tell you to do."

"What happened to you after the lion attack? You have never asked for my opinion before, or when I could do something you wanted me to do – you'd usually just tell me what to do and I'd do it."

"This is different, son. I can tell you to do a chore, but I cannot tell you to live a life. Living life successfully is a matter of your desire, your willingness to change and your willingness to learn what you are being taught, not only by me but by anybody who is good at what they do."

Sani was now sure that his son would come on board, so he continued. "So do I have your answer?"

"Baba, I will do whatever you request of me. I am excited to hear what your idea is about."

"I will not tell you the entire idea – you have to experience it as you go along. It is part of exposing you to the things that will make you successful."

"OK. When do we start?"

"Your food is getting cold. Eat; we will begin tomorrow at dawn. We will take a walk and I will tell you more."

The two men ate the rest of the traditional deer stew mixed with green vegetables, complemented by thickened cornmeal and sweet potatoes. They drank water to cap the feeding process. It was an afternoon that left Tindo's mind running about in many directions. Excitement and fear conflicted in many respects. He, however, had faith in his father; history had proven that nothing his father asked of him would be impossible to do or accomplish.

CHAPTER THREE

GO FISH WHEN OTHERS GO HUNT

Four months into the summer, it had become apparent that the drought season had visited Zimuto. A month before that day, the chief had ordered some reserved corn inventories to be released to the community strategically on a monthly basis. Emphasis was placed on families to be very responsible with their rations. More and more young men were learning to hunt because hunting had become the number one source of livelihood for most families. The process was simple, it went as follows: bring a beast, take half for your family and trade the other half in exchange for firewood, vegetables and other valuable commodities. The more beasts you brought home, the more trading power you had for other commodities. Some people had mastered the skill of using the new government currency to trade with others. Some savvy villagers went to the city to work, brought back bread and sold it from makeshift tuck shops.

Sani and his family were now feeling the pinch because Sani had not been able to hunt in a long time. To make matters worse, he instructed his son Tee to go fishing instead of hunting.

"Baba, I know we have a plan, but things have changed in the past three months." Tindo tried to convince his dad to let him go hunting with his friends instead. "I can bring a beast a week. Look at Shepherd, he has half my hunting skill but he is bringing home a beast every two weeks."

"I said no! This family will not settle for leftovers when it can cook the whole meal." Sani reprimanded his son in an angry tone.

"Ba—"

Sani immediately stood up. "Enough!"

His son, who was thinking that the family was already settling for leftovers as nobody was out catching beasts, got the message and shut his mouth before uttering another word. In those days, when the head of the household became upset, nobody opened their mouth; otherwise, it would be interpreted as a sign of disrespect. So Tee sat quietly until his father released him. He went straight to his hut and closed the door. His mother overhead the noise and saw Tee walking grudgingly across the compound. She walked across and saw her husband sitting on a wooden stool with his face wrapped in his hands, so she opened a conversation with him softly. "Masikati Baba Tee?" She greeted him in their native language.

"Afternoon, Mai Tee."

"Are you all right? Is everything all right?"

"Not exactly, Mai Tee." He beckoned her to sit next to him. "I instructed Tee to go fishing with Mr. Hove but he keeps arguing with me about going hunting with his friends instead."

Mai Tee did not respond so Sani continued. "He knows what we agreed on. He must follow through or else we will not achieve the goal."

"I think I know what he is going through," his wife commented.

Sani stared at her but did not interrupt her. "Every mother in the village is insulting me, implying that we are irresponsible for not having our son hunt, and yet expect them to share food with us."

"I have not asked for anything from anybody!" Sani angrily responded.

"I know, Baba Tee," Mai Tee calmly replied. "However, that is what is being said. Tee has heard it through his friends. They are mocking him for being a coward who cannot live up to his father's reputation. They boast that they are bringing two, at times three beasts home while he is sweeping his mother's yard."

Sani kept quiet as he processed the rather provocative remarks coming from the Zimuto community.

"Baba Tee, everybody thinks we are beggars who no longer possess the attitude to work for our own livelihood. Is there anything you can do to spare us this embarrassment?"

"Mai Tee, our predecessors once said that the man who laughs last has the best laugh. Let them laugh... they are bringing what, one or two beasts? We will be bringing twenty or thirty a day. People will always mock anybody who takes a different approach from the majority; that does not make them right. Our results will exonerate us. But we can only achieve our big goal if we focus on our plan. We cannot afford to run just because things have become tougher and people are laughing at us. Let them do that; I assure you that they will be embarrassed to come and ask for food at our house," Sani explained, looking into his wife's eyes.

Mai Tee believed him. After all, this was the man she had been married to for over two decades. She knew when he was serious, and when he was right. This time, he was both serious and right.

"You are right, my husband. Even waters in rivers pass through rocky ground, through falls and heavy sands before they reach the ocean. You have my full support. I will speak to our boy if you do not mind," Mai Tee said.

"Thank you, my wife."

Funny how a small dose of support and encouragement from a loved one fuels the human drive. Sani's mood had clearly turned the corner; his face was now straight and his body was full of energy.

"Let me talk to him, Mai Tee. I need him to know I am proud of him," Sani said as he got up to walk towards Tee's hut.

After spending a few minutes with his son, speaking from the heart and discussing their plan in more detail, Sani left Tee's hut even more assured his son was on board with his grand plan.

The Fishing Trip ...

The air was dry on a Monday morning, and a fresh breeze belted Tee's face as he made his way to Mr. Hove's house. The day for the much-anticipated fishing trip had arrived and he seemed ready for the trip to end before it even began. He was going on the trip to please his father, but Tee was still struggling with the idea of how the trip would be better than the village's popular hunting getaways that his age-mates were now accustomed to. Before he crossed the dry Runde River, Tee overhead voices coming from his right side. He looked in the direction and he saw a group of young women taking turns to scoop the last of the water that was yet to evaporate from the dark sands of the river because of high temperatures and lack of rain. To his surprise, the group had noticed his presence long before he recognized them. Tee discovered he was the subject of discussion. As if he could not hear a word, the ladies continued to talk without looking in his direction. It was obvious they thought he was long gone.

"Tee has become an embarrassment to his family and this community," one of the ladies said before another voiced in.

"To think that this is the man we were all fighting to marry just three months ago! What a shame."

"My father told me he is a coward, and he would never accept any of his daughters to get married to a coward."

"Do you really believe he is a coward?" Chipo, the soft-spoken voice among the group, and also a young woman of unmistakable physical beauty, spoke up eventually.

"Chipo, I am beginning to think that you are deaf. Why do you always side with cowards?"

"I cannot imagine Sani having raised a coward. He is the greatest warrior this land has seen yet. I saw Tee wrestle at the summer celebrations, and he beat every young man he fought against. I did not see fear in his eyes, did you, Tina?"

"I don't look in the eyes of cowards," Tina replied as she raised her head to look directly in the direction that Tee was standing. Their eyes connected the same moment that the entire group realized Tee had been listening to the most damning part of their conversation. After casting another angry glance at the group, Tee began walking towards Mr. Hove's compound. Many thoughts ran through his head as he tried to make sense of his newly discovered reputation. The shame rested on his head like a dead elephant. His step was now labored and full of doubt. It was not long before he reached the entrance of Mr. Hove's compound. Three men, including Mr. Hove, were sitting and chatting quietly under a tree when Tee arrived. Clearly he was late, so he apologized before the men began their journey to the south village rivers. Mr. Hove's four hunting dogs were leading the way along a dusty path.

After a two-hour walk the men reached the first waterhole. They quickly noticed that half the water had evaporated and the banks were overcrowded with people and animals trying to get their share of the remaining water. Before long the group had concluded that the waterhole was not the best source of healthy fish. Just as quickly as it ended, the journey to look for another, and hopefully better waterhole, began once again.

Mr. Hove and his crew of three men, which included Tee, had been hiking for five hours going from waterhole to waterhole along rivers located in the southern valley of Zimuto. Eventually they reached the banks of dark-colored waters protected by a rocky mountain range and tall Mopani trees. Tee had not seen such dark and deep waters since the drought season began. It was clear the waterhole was protected from most wild animals by the enormous rocks surrounding it.

It was extremely difficult to access the banks of the waterhole. The group of men had to climb over several large rocks in order to get near the water.

"Now I see why nobody ever comes to Mvuu waterhole," Mr. Hove commented wiping sweat off his forehead. "It is almost impossible for anything to access these waters because of the rocks surrounding them."

"Is that why there are no animals inside the waterhole drinking water?" Tee asked.

"Precisely," Mr. Hove responded as he surveyed the banks of the waterhole.

The men finally identified a convenient spot for fishing. They began to prepare their rods, coiling worms around the hooks that would be used to bait fish into their life-ending trap. The process was intriguing, but rather boring for an energetic young man of Tee's caliber. However, by sundown the men had caught three sacks of fish.

"We will set up camp one kilometer this way," said Mr. Hove. "Tee, you have a sack all to yourself, very impressive for your first fishing trip."

"I was just lucky, Mr. Hove," Tee replied.

"There is no luck in fishing, my child. You either catch or you don't."

The crew walked in a single line following a previously travelled trail that ran parallel to a river. Mr. Hove led the way, followed by one other man; Tee was third in line. Suddenly, the crew's dogs started barking, and Mr. Hove instructed them to shut it. As they looked ahead, the tall grass seemed to be moving in a parting fashion towards them. The dogs continued barking furiously, and instantly Mr. Hove sensed that they were all in great danger.

"Run, gentlemen, run!" he shouted as he turned to run in the direction they were coming from.

Immediately the men took off like cheetahs. Tee, being the youngest, was also the fastest. He hesitated running too far ahead of the group for fear of running into oncoming danger, so he glanced behind them as he heard one of the dogs begin to growl soundly to indicate it had been attacked by something. Mr. Hove pointed at the rocks to their left.

"Let's head for the rocks, people, do not look behind or you will trip and fall," he explained as he went through the tall, dry grass.

After a short run, all of the men and three of their dogs had made it safely to the top of the balancing rocks of Mvuu waterhole. It was at that moment that they discovered their entire day's catch was missing. So was New York, Mr. Hove's most prized dog, given to him by a visiting missionary from the United States of America. The missionary had told him stories about the city of New York just before his favorite dog delivered a litter. Mr. Hove was gifted a puppy, which he named "New York." As the men looked down into the grass to make sense of what had been chasing them, it became clear that they were running from an adult hippo.

"How did you know danger was coming?" asked Tee.

"We are close to water and many people have been attacked around this waterhole by hippos. That is the reason why this waterhole is called Mvuu, after the ugly animal" said Mr. Hove.

Finally, the dark brown, wide-mouthed animal reached the edge of the rock that the men had climbed on. Its mouth was bloody, showing evidence of the fate of New York. The hippo seemed restless and panted back and forth in a cheeky manner as if to warn the men that they had crossed the line this time around.

"Why did we come to a waterhole where there are hippos?" Tee asked.

"Because it is the best waterhole for fish at this time of the year," Mr. Hove replied. "Since we have been here, we have not witnessed any people fishing the same waters."

Mvuu waterhole was a large body of dark waters; it was deep and also a very popular spot for wild birds to flock and sing. Mvuu was also unusual because grazers, due to the rocky hills surrounding them, could not access the waters, and therefore were absent. Hippos made it their home for the peace and other reasons.

"Tee, hippos love this waterhole because they are not disturbed by large numbers of animals, especially grazers coming to quench their thirst." Mr. Hove volunteered to the youngest member of their group.

After about five minutes, the hippo left; trotting towards the water. The group saw it enter and disappear underneath the body of water.

"We need our gear for camping and food," one of the men said quietly.

So the men hesitantly went down and into the grass in search of their possessions. They began to pick up everything, one by one until they found the sacks of fish and their camping gear. The men fetched some water and firewood before going back to the rocks to cook and sleep.

After another full day of fishing, the group visited two more waterholes, but none of them were as productive as Mvuu waterhole. So they made their way back home on the fourth day of the trip. Mr. Hove was not happy about the loss of one of his dogs, although he was impressed by Tee's ability to adapt to different situations. The men exchanged stories of heroism throughout the journey, and at dusk, they reached their respective homes.

CHAPTER FOUR

FIND A WATERHOLE AND FENCE IT

When Tee arrived home, his father was sitting by a fire and eating roasted nuts.

"Welcome home, my child," Sani said as he rose to greet his son, who seemed to be struggling with two wet sacks of fish.

"Makadii Baba?" Tee greeted his father traditionally.

"Very well, my boy; did you have a pleasant time?"

"Yes, except for a hippo incident."

Tee went on to narrate the main events of the trip and how he caught the fish he brought home. The two men were joined by Tee's mother and sisters as suppertime was officially on for the family. Tee's animations made the entire family chuckle and his story about the hippo did not particularly please his mother. After two hours, members of Sani's family were sleeping soundly on their mats enjoying their well-deserved rest.

When Tee woke up the next morning, his mother and sisters had finished salting the fish and laid it to dry on a hand-built shed. The smell of fresh fish attracted a lot of flies, but the smoke set around the shed prevented the flies from reaching the fish.

"This is your work, Tee," his mother complimented him as he approached.

"Thank you, mother, where is baba?" Tee asked.

"Inside his hut, waiting for you to get up," his mother replied. "Your tea is served and I know your father will not begin before you get in."

Tee quickly strode towards his father's hut. He knew instantly that Sani had something important to discuss by the way things were arranged.

"There is my oldest." Sani smiled as he addressed his son.

"Morning, Baba." Tee greeted his dad.

"Morning to you too, my son, let me pour you a cup of tea."

"Thank you, Baba." Tee extended his hand to get the cup.

Sani immediately opened the conversation. "So tell me about the waterholes you visited."

"We visited seven in total, Baba; however, Mvuu was the largest and we had our biggest catch there."

"It was the biggest, but were there many people?"

"No, we were the only humans there, but flocks of birds

came in from every direction, Baba," Tee explained. "I have never seen such a variety of bird species in one place."

"Are you serious?" Sani asked, probing his son to continue explaining.

"Yes, there were swallows, martins, eagles, stork and hundreds of small birds."

"Did you see any predators?"

"No, except obviously we encountered a hippo," Tee narrated. "Mr. Hove seemed to like the waters but said he would not be back due to the hippo incident."

"I know, they are dangerous; Hippos kill the most humans in Zimuto," Sani explained to Tee.

"Really?" Tee asked for confirmation.

"Yes, more than lions, hyenas and leopards."

Sani took a sip from his cup of tea and continued. "Was the grass green?"

"Yes, on most sides, except on the side we settled to fish." Tee described the grasslands surrounding the Mvuu Waterhole.

"Son, well done; I thought it would take you several trips to find a fitting waterhole, but you did it in one trip," Sani said while getting up.

In a surprising turn of events, Sani broke into a dance, kicking his feet one by one forward and swinging his hands in a co-ordinated fashion. Tee sat there surprised and wondering what the dance was all about.

"It's a victory dance, son... join me if you want."

"No thanks, Baba." Tee wisely turned down the invitation.

Sani stopped, turned around and said to Tee, "God has led you to the family's hunting ground."

Tee was plainly confused and did not say a word.

"You found the waterhole, son," Sani began explaining.

"Baba, I am confused. Are you happy about the fish or the waterhole?" Tee asked.

"The fish... no! I mean yes, I'm also happy about your catch, but I am delighted about your discovery of Mvuu waterhole," Sani tried to answer his son.

"I am not sure you understand. There are hippos at Mvuu, not a single grazer and nobody is going back fishing over there, not even Mr. Hove himself." Tee tried to reiterate the facts to his father.

"Then we leave after tomorrow for Mvuu," Sani said, extending his hand towards Tee's shoulder. "I heard you, son."

"So why do you want to go there again?" Tee asked.

"My words cannot make you understand fully my intent, but you will know as we build this plan further, my boy."

The next day, Sani was at Chief Gato's home requesting for a cart to take him and some warriors to the waterhole. Chief did not understand Sani's plan either but he had learned to accept Sani's requests over the years. As a matter of fact, he wanted to sit Sani down to talk about Tee's absence in the hunting grounds of Zimuto, but Sani did not have time to talk.

A day later, four warriors, Tee and his father were riding in the same cart on their way to Mvuu waterhole. After a half-day ride, they arrived. In their approach the men witnessed a marvel of wild animals socializing around the mountains. It was clear they could smell the fresh water but they could not find a way through the mountain rocks protecting Mvuu waterhole. It was a sight of herbivores of varying sizes and types. The grazers did not seem to care that humans were approaching. One warrior took his bow and arrow and aimed it in the direction of a healthy deer, but Sani quickly stopped him from releasing the arrow.

"You do that, you scare the lot," Sani explained. "We are here to just look around and find where to create an entrance into the waterhole."

"Entrance?" Tee asked with confusion in his tone.

"Yes, I will explain later," Sani replied as he directed the cart towards the shade owned by a pair of Mopani trees.

The men spent three hours walking around the waterhole and analyzing the perimeter. Sani told everyone to put wooden markers around the perimeter so that they could remember when they returned. While inside, and near the water, Tee could not believe he was at the very spot that he had encountered the hippo a week earlier.

"What's that smell?" Sani asked.

"New York, Baba, this is where he was killed."

"Huh?" It was Sani's turn to be confused.

"That's the name of Mr. Hove's dog," Tee explained.

45

"Oh, the one who was attacked?"

"Yes."

When the men finished their investigation, they began watching the animals and talking about the types of grazers they could recognize. Not long after that, they began their journey back home. Tee could not believe how stubborn his father was being. He could not understand why they were riding a cattle-drawn cart through the bush, between trees and over grass in hippo land.

As if he had read his son's mind, Sani said, "We are using the cart to create a trail for when we return."

"What?" Tee muttered, but nobody responded to him.

Tee was most annoyed that the warriors seemed to enjoy the whole adventure. For the first time he hated the way the warriors respected, believed and obeyed his father. He thought they had become insane. If only he had a choice, this would be his last trip to Mvuu waterhole. After a few hours circling the outside perimeter of the mountain range, Sani identified what would be the entrance to the waterhole.

"This will do. Do you see how that huge rock is supported by soil from the inside?" Sani asked his warrior friends, but nobody answered as they were still trying to figure out what he had discovered.

"Please peg this length." Sani pointed out a distance of about fifty meters. "We are going to fence this whole space and erect the fence against those rocks to the right, and that huge granite to the left."

"Why do we need to fence it?" Tee asked.

"In order to protect the waterhole," Sani quickly explained to his son.

Cutting Poles...

A week later Tee woke up to voices of men speaking outside his hut. It was just after the roosters had crowed, and the day was still dark with a promise of dawn showing in the horizon towards the east. He rose from his mat, tossed his blankets and opened his door.

The twins and his father were chatting away. The twins were sons of Mbira, a Zimuto man skilled in building thatched huts. The two boys had adopted their father's trade and were already known for their construction skills around Zimuto.

"Here he is." One of the twins pointed at Tee.

"What are you doing here? Do you need help building anything?" Tee asked as he remembered his days helping the brothers cut logs for construction.

"We are here to help you and your dad cut some poles, Tee."

Immediately Tee remembered his father mentioning it the day before. He just had no idea it would be that early. As the discussion went on, five other men arrived with their axes. Then another set of men arrived, and by sunrise, Tee had lost count of the number of men who had come to help with cutting poles at his father's request. It became apparent that most of the men were warriors of Zimuto who had come with their sons. After a short briefing by Sani, they all set out in different directions to cut poles of at least Sani's height. For a week the men continued the process of cutting poles and taking them to Mvuu waterhole. The poles were strategically placed around the proposed entrance in a manner that enabled quick assembly.

Tee noticed that most animals arrived around noon and spent about three hours at the waterhole before heading back into the forest thirsty, some dying of dehydration on the side of the mountains. On the other side of the rock-filled mountains, he noticed that the hippos spent most of their time in the water playing with each other. He also noticed that most of the men helping his father had no clue what his plan was. They simply obeyed orders and enjoyed a drink of home-brewed grain drink. Being a quick mind himself, Tee realized that his dad wanted a fence built around the waterhole entrance to control activity inside the waterhole. Maybe the drought would prolong and the water would become essential to human life, he thought.

After three weeks of hard, coordinated work, the fence was erected around the waterhole's proposed entrance. It extended beyond the dimensions for the entrance, enclosing a large area of grazing land. A large wooden gate was built at the site. It was very wide and adjoined the pole fence, making it impossible for anything to reach the waterhole when the gate was closed. After all the work was done, Sani thanked the crew just before they headed to their respective homes.

CHAPTER FIVE

MOVE ROCKS AND LET GRAZERS IN

In the weekend following the erection of the fence, Zimuto was celebrating a "Feast of Provisions." This was an event of giving thanks to God for providing food during a season of scarcity. During the main night, bonfires were lit at Hondo Valley, on the south side of Zimuto. Most of the citizens of Zimuto were gathered there in groups separated by age and gender. Tee was sitting with his peers listening to Jona tell stories about his hunting successes. Jona had become the talk of Zimuto and had seemingly displaced Tee as the most eligible bachelor in the village.

The discussion heated up when Chipo and a group of girls arrived at the bonfire for young men with some roasted meat. Upon recognizing the presence of new company, one young man shouted, "Jona, tell us how you brought two beasts home this past week."

"It was not a problem at all. I learned from my mentor, Sani, that a real man should never be taken hostage by fear," Jona arrogantly muttered.

Immediately Tee's eyebrows rose in response to Jona's statement. Tee, who was sitting directly across from Jona, separated only by the burning fire, noticed that Jona was trying to impress the young women who had brought them food.

"My father never said that," Tee responded in a stern voice while waving smoke from his face.

"Even if he didn't, he showed it by his bravery." Jona poked at Tee again.

"Is this about my father or about me?" Tee asked Jona.

"These are men stories, Tee. We are talking about hunting, not fishing," Jona loudly proclaimed and the crowd responded with massive laughter.

As the laughter subsided, Tee leaped through the flames onto Jona's throat and dragged him to the ground. Immediately, the other young men jumped to pull Tee from Jona. Tee was now sitting on Jona's chest, his left hand on his throat and his right hand raised to strike at Jona's jaw. Four young men pulled Tee aside and stood between him and Jona, who was now lying on the ground gasping for air.

The sound of young women screaming and young men shouting drew the attention of Sani and the chief's guests, seated around a bonfire about forty meters away. The men rushed to where the noise was coming from. Upon his arrival, Sani discovered his son was in the middle of it all and another young man was lying on the ground breathing heavily.

Sani soon learned what had happened and reprimanded his son. However, deep down inside he had opposite feelings about his son's participation in the incident. As a matter of fact, Mai Tee noticed Sani's silent pleasure when the two arrived home later that night; she was not amused by either man.

"If you want to fight everyone who speaks ill of you, then you must start with our neighbors tomorrow and go through every household of Zimuto," Mai Tee angrily addressed her son.

"Sorry Mai," Tee apologized.

"Baba Tee, you are not ashamed of this?"

"Aah, yes, it is very upsetting," Sani said as he fought to hold back suppressed laughter.

Mai Tee pointed at the door and Tee left immediately. Sani also got the message, so he also went to sleep from there.

Another trip to Mvuu waterhole...

Two days after the incident, a group of fifty men assembled at Sani's compound ready to make another trip to Mvuu. They brought with them eight strong bulls yoked together and ready to pull any size load. As previously planned, they were going at Sani's request. Tee was among the men who were assembling carts to get the journey started. Not long after that, the men were on their way, cart after cart.

Mvuu waterhole looked different from the last time Tee was there. A well-built wooden fence structure now protected a portion of it. Sani began to explain the plan for the day.

"Gentlemen, we will be creating an entrance into the waterhole behind this gate. I want the first ten men to begin digging out the soil beneath the biggest granite rock. We will make use of the plough in order to expedite the process. The bulls will help pull the trees around the crop of rocks on the right. I am hoping that once we dig deep enough, the rock's weight and a little push from us will cause it to move downhill, pushing all the other obstacles out of the way."

"Let's go, men of Zimuto," one warrior shouted while waiving at the group.

It took about seven hours of digging before the large rock began to show signs of movement.

"Now get out of the way!" shouted Sani. "It's time to push the rock down the mountain!"

The men began to push, with very little noticeable movement. They dug a little more and got back to pushing the big rock. After a few minutes of trying, the rock slowly began to move, and then stopped. Silence followed for a minute and then Sani began to make his way towards the big rock in order to inspect the reason why it had stopped sliding. Sani simply touched the giant rock and it immediately began moving again; this time it moved to the right, pushing all the small rocks out of the way and it returned a little before it began sliding downhill. At first its movement was slow, but it gained momentum and began crushing rocks and trees that tried to stop it from going towards the water. Finally it accelerated all the way into the waterhole, which was about a half a kilometer away. When it touched the waterhole, it displaced such a large amount of water that the hippos feasting a good distance away began to swim away.

The water regained its calmness but nobody could see the rock.

"Where is the rock?" Tee asked in surprise.

"Underneath the water, son; It is a deep waterhole," Sani replied.

The group stood in the large, open gap behind the gate, admiring the ripple waves created by the big rock when it hit the water. Birds had long taken to the sky and small rodents could be seen running along the banks of the waterhole, possibly thinking the sky had fallen. After a few minutes of watching various events unfold, the group began to clear all the trees and small rocks to make the way to the waterhole flat. Sani spoke after about an hour, this time at the edge of water.

"Did we leave the gate closed up there?"

"Yes we did," one of the warriors responded while searching for souvenir stones.

"OK. Let's all take a knee in thanksgiving," Sani said as one of his knees touched the wet sand on the shores of Mvuu waterhole.

The group prayed and began walking around the waterhole. Tee was on the lookout for hippos, but none could be seen nearby.

"I had no idea the waterhole was this deep; I can only see a tiny tip of the big rock below the clear water," Tee stated.

"Neither did I; this rock was bigger than my two huts put together," one warrior commented.

At dusk, the men found a place to camp and were sound asleep on top of mountain rocks in no time. The following dawn, Sani instructed that the gates be left open for the next week.

"Take the hay in the carts and sprinkle it to where the wild animals will come in search of water." Sani gave orders. "Also take the fresh hay to the other end of mountains and make sure that it leaves a trail back to this waterhole entrance. I also want hay placed all the way down to the waterhole."

One week later...

Tee could not believe his eyes as they approached the waters again. At midday, thousands of animals had taken residence inside the fence. A clear majority of them were grazers, but there were still a sizeable lot of small predators. Many were drinking water and quenching their thirst of many days, perhaps weeks for others.

Sani instructed all the men to stand at a distance and quietly observe everything the grazers were doing. They noticed, after about two hours, that mass numbers of grazers began leaving the fence enclosure in search of pastures. Only a handful of animals remained around the waterhole by sunset. Sani ordered the gate closed. The men made their way to the rocks to camp for the night. The next morning everyone in the group sat and waited for the animals to come. A little after mid-morning, the animals began arriving in large numbers. The unfortunate part for them was that the gate was closed, just as Sani wanted.

After a large population of grazers had occupied the outskirts of the fence, Sani ordered the gate to be opened so that grazers could come in.

"We need to chase away all the animals not fit for human consumption," one of the men said.

"If you attempt to do that, you will either get trampled by the animals or you will chase the entire herd away. I want the herd of grazers in the fence. Other animals are part of the experience. As long as we do not get lions here, we will be all right," Sani explained.

When the gate sprung open, the animals muscled their way in and headed for the water. Their numbers had increased from the previous day.

"Why do we keep opening and closing the gate, Baba?" Tee inquired.

"We are training grazers to know that there is one entrance to the water and that there is no danger inside the fence," Sani responded.

Sani stood gazing at the still water and began scratching his head. His son noticed there was something wrong, so he asked, "What's the problem, Baba?"

"Oh, I am thinking of a way to keep the animals inside for days as opposed to hours," Sani answered.

"Well, why don't you just close the gate?" Tee asked again.

"If we do that, the moment we open that gate, the grazers will go and will not return in big numbers. You never want to force them into staying; they must voluntarily make this their home," Sani explained.

"How do you do that then?" Tee continued his questioning.

"I guess that is the reason I am scratching my head."

The group laughed and started walking back to their carts. The other men wanted to catch a beast or two but Sani denied them the opportunity.

"I am not happy about one thing," Sani said as he squeezed through two trees to get to his cart. "Did you also notice that only a handful of young grazers could drink water?"

"Yes!" the men responded in unison, sounding like a choir.

"That is another problem that needs fixing," Sani said.

Nobody responded, implying that they had no idea why that problem needed fixing. Shortly, the group realized that their shadows were now long and pointing east, meaning that the sun was now setting. The men quickly began their journey back to their families.

CHAPTER SIX

GET THE HERD TO STAY LONGER

Again Sani and his ten warrior friends were at Mvuu waterhole. This time they had a solution to get the grazers to stay longer each time they visited. It did not take long before the men set out to work, creating furrows that ran away from the waterhole and the attached river. Almost immediately after the meandering furrows were created, the water began to flow along the shallow trenches. Within two hours, a significant swamp had started to form.

"Why are we creating a swamp along the banks?" asked a confused Tee.

"You see, my son, adult grazers can drink straight from

deep waters, but their young cannot. They are dying of thirst and their mothers have no way of helping. However, once the mothers see the swamps, they will take their babies to drink from shallow waters," his father shared.

"I see; so once the young grazers are on the southern side, their mothers will stay."

"For a while they will. once the young have a reason to stay, their mothers will have a reason to stay, and when the females stay, so will all the eligible male grazers," Sani said, continuing to school his son.

"But without grazing pastures, they will not stay that long, Baba."

"I agree; however, the swamps will give rise to green pastures and that will cause a lot of grazers to maintain camp within the fence. We will also throw in some salty sand, which grazers love to lick, and each week we will bring corn chuff from the ration storehouses. Corn chuff is a delicacy in the grazer world." The father outlined the plan.

"Yes, if there is one thing I know grazers will stay for, it is corn chuff, because I grew tired of chasing multiple herds from our fields last year," Tee recalled.

So the men continued until it was dark before they setup camp nearby. The next morning Chief Gato and his delegation arrived at Mvuu waterhole. An excited Sani greeted them and began showing them around. Tee could see the pride in his father's eyes, but he was yet to fully comprehend the impact of the project on the entire community of Zimuto. The chief seemed equally excited as he surveyed the rather large perimeter outlined by the fence.

"So when do you start?" Chief asked.

"In two weeks, after the pastures have taken shape," Sani responded.

"You have made me proud, my friend. My father was right about you; he kept telling me you would do great things one day, so I should stick around you." The Chief was now reminiscing about his predecessor.

As expected, Sani dismissed the chief's statement and began making arrangements for the delivery of the salty sand to the waterhole as if he had not been touched by the compliment. At the same time, little did Tee know that two weeks from that day, things would begin to change in a mighty way in the land of Zimuto.

It was an incredible sight to most men standing with Sani that afternoon. Half of the grazers had not even left the fence since arriving the day before. Hundreds more began to filter in slowly, arriving and making the entire waterhole a very congested place. More and more female grazers began to cross the shallow feeder river to the southern side with their calves. Not long after, some male counterparts began to follow the train.

"Just as you said, Sani," one of the warriors commented.

"The grazers are making their way to the southern side because of the swamp."

Sani smiled and let the scene acknowledge the comment. It felt really exciting, Sani thought to himself – thought can indeed turn into reality. All it takes is committed effort and a unique strategy. Soon after, the men departed for their homes. They agreed on a plan to return after a week.

Luck follows results...

Sani and his son were approaching their compound when they noticed his wife walking in their direction in the company of a man. As they drew closer, they recognized Sani's brother-in-law.

"We were beginning to wonder if you were coming back today," his wife said.

"Why?"

"It's almost end of day and I have been here since morning," his brother-in-law complained politely.

"It must be important for you to wait that long," Sani remarked as the men pulled up stools to sit in a semi-circle fashion under a guest shed built by Sani.

"I will get straight to the point because I have to journey back home in a few minutes," Tee's uncle said. "A government officer came to the school yesterday and asked if I knew someone who could open and run a butchery. I told them I did and that person was Sani."

"I do not want to insult you, but what is a butchery?" Sani queried, as a stern expression overtook his face.

"Oh, it is a store that sells meat only. My thinking was that since you know the most about grazers and cattle in this village, you would be the best person to run it," his brother-in-law continued.

"Baba, in light of what..."

Sani quickly raised his hand to silence his son from talking further.

"I will do it," Sani responded to his brother-in-law.

"You will?"

"I believe I just said so. Who will build the butchery?" Sani asked.

"The government will pay people to do it; they just want to know who will run it."

"Tell the government that I will build my own butchery, but they can train Tee and me," Sani responded with his eyebrows raised.

"The government will accept anything that saves them money. Your proposition saves them thousands," Sani's brother-in-law cheerfully explained.

"OK. You and I must go and see the chief tomorrow to explain this new plan. Tee, inform the twins that we will need their help to build the butchery. You are my real friend, uncle. I thought your kindness would end after you gave me your sister, but it keeps flowing. Thank you." Sani stood and shook his brother-in-law's hand.

S. GABRIEL SHUMBA

Sani convinced his brother-in-law to spend the night. His excitement spread across his face in evidence of his pleasant mood. He explained to Tee the importance of this new addition to their existing plan. The men exchanged ideas and laughter over a delicious supper of pumpkin leaves with fish and corn-meal sadza. Mai Tee joined the conversation and the four kept at it until it was time to go and rest. At the crack of dawn, Sani went to see the chief with his brother-in-law; before long, work on cutting the logs for constructing a new butchery began.

It was now almost two weeks since Sani and his team had last been to the waterhole. They decided to go again. Upon their arrival, they noticed that the southern side was now greener and more animals were staying inside the fence longer. Some were spending days inside. The salty sand was all licked up and the men could tell that the animals were now comfortable with the environment they were in. The fence boundary no longer looked exotic; it was now a part of familiar surroundings to the animals. On that day, the men kept their distance, stayed for two hours and then left again.

Sani addressed the group of about a dozen men just before they departed the valleys of Mvuu waterhole. "Gentlemen, we will meet at my compound in two days. Come prepared to hunt; our time has come. God has visited us in a mighty way."

CHAPTER SEVEN

GO HUNT AT THE WATERHOLE

News had been spreading for weeks around Zimuto about Sani and his warrior group. The village word was that Sani had been trying to hunt for over a month and had not been lucky. Others began to mock his family, saying they were going hunting in the waters, instead of the mountains where brave men had been going. Sani and his family ignored the gossip because they knew the plan they were pursuing. He often remarked to his wife, son and fellow warriors that they were after a plan and their results would exonerate them, not their words. His regular blurbs of inspiration kept his followers committed and optimistic. After all, if anyone was to bet against Sani, they were likely to lose big in the end.

Two days prior, Sani and his group had crossed paths with another group of men going on their way to a three-day hunting trip. They exchanged greetings but their glances revealed more about their thoughts towards Sani's group than did their words. Sani's hope was that they would meet again on their way back.

Sani's group arrived at Mvuu waterhole around mid-morning on that day and everything was as they had left it two days before. In excitement, the warriors began sharpening their spears against rocky edges.

"It looks like we do not need any bow and arrows today," one of them said as he sharpened his spear.

"Listen, gentlemen, we only need one specialized spear today. Tee already has it and he will do the work. It is a pin-shaped spear that is very thin and is stuffed at the tip with muti herb, our traditional tranquilizer," Sani explained to the group. "We will put salt and hay into the wooden tunnel that leads to the entrance. The animals that come through will walk along this wooden tunnel and as they reach the end, Tee will prick them on the neck one by one. They will not feel a thing but will drop after walking a further fifty meters. At that time I want you to take the beast and treat it in the usual hunting manner before you put it in the cart."

"That sounds even easier than I thought. I had been wondering why we built the short tunnel facing the southern gate," one satisfied warrior commented.

"Let the work begin, gentlemen," Sani ordered.

All the men took their pre-assigned positions. Tee and another man carrying the can of muti herb went to sit by the tunnel behind the wooden poles. They were barely visible to the animals walking inside the tunnel. The other warriors stood about fifty meters away from the end of the short tunnel. Sani climbed a tree and sat patiently along one of the branches. He waved at the man at the gate and instantly, the gate began to open. At first no animal walked out; after about ten minutes, two grazers began the walk through the gate into the short tunnel and out into the open. By the time they reached the open area, Tee had already done his job and both beasts fell down within meters of each other. The warriors on standby rushed to pull them from sight and slaughtered them next to the carts before heaving them inside. The process continued for a while until all the carts were filled with beasts. Sani counted twenty-five grazers that had been slaughtered.

"Enough for today," Sani shouted as he jumped down from the tree he had been resident in for the past hour.

The excited warriors began to whistle and jump in victorious jubilation. Nobody had ever been able to catch twenty-five beasts in an hour, not in the land of Zimuto and nearby villages. Yet Sani and his helpers did it, without using spears or bows and arrows. So the men proudly left, walking behind their respective carts as there was no more room to sit inside. As if heaven had a plan, Sani's team met up again with the group they had seen three days earlier. That group was pulling one beast of a much smaller size. In three days, their work had been hard, risky and all four were to share the single beast.

The men stood like statues as their eyes revealed the large number of beasts in the carts belonging to Sani's group.

"Which hunting grounds are you coming from, Baba Tee?" Their leader addressed Sani using a more respectful traditional reference.

"These did not come from any hunting grounds, my fellow villagers; they came from our fence," Sani responded in a proud voice.

He could tell the men did not get it. However, this was not the time to stand and educate them because Sani was looking forward to the expression on his wife's face when she would see the beasts he was bringing home. Sani extended an invitation to the weary hunters to come to his house for a village feast a week away, where he promised to explain everything to them. He then left with his entourage.

Joy at the compound...

Mai Tee had gotten used to the sight of seeing several carts approach her compound since Sani and Tee began going to the waterhole. On this day the sight was different. All the men were walking, but the carts were full with something she could not describe from her standing distance. Her two girls and a group of female guests joined her because the sight did not make sense to them either.

"Beasts! Amai, they are carrying beasts," one of her daughters was shouting in excitement.

"You are right, my daughter, they are beasts," Mai Tee spoke back in a surprised tone.

As the carts approached, followed by twelve men, the human noise of excitement began to increase. The female guests were the wives of Sani's warriors who had been requested by their respective husbands to wait for them at Sani's compound for an important meeting. For most of the day, they had no idea what the meeting was about until they discovered what their eyes incorrectly interpreted as a hundred beasts in the men's carts, arriving at Sani's compound. Tee could not hold back his emotions, so he sprinted into his mother's arms.

Women ululated in expression of their joy. Every other wife embraced her husband, tears of joy flowing down their faces. Sani's daughters were all over him because the occasion was that important. The family's ridicule, rejection, insult and bad reputation in the community had all but vanished in one incident. God had indeed visited Sani's family and wealth had befallen them in a great and dramatic way. Indeed this was evidence that favor can restore in a day what was lost in a lifetime. The celebration continued into the night, with one beast being at the center of the feast of fortune in Sani's home. Finally, the group dispersed and went to sleep inside Sani's compound.

The next morning - all the ladies were up early, gutting the beasts, and salting and smoking the meat. When the men got up, they began to help; it was all smiles around Sani's place. The news travelled faster than lightning and the entire village had heard that Sani had a plan after all. Most were not surprised, even though they participated in the gossip.

After the guests had left, Mai Tee continued to express her surprise and pride towards her husband and son. She could not believe that from then onwards, whenever she needed anything, she could simply send her husband and son to the fence to get a beast. It had become that easy.

"Mai Tee, think of whatever you need, and we will go and get a beast to trade for it," Sani told his wife.

"I have everything I need for now, my husband," she responded in a grateful tone.

"Why do you keep staring at me like that?" Sani asked his wife.

She expressed her thoughts. "I cannot believe that this is exactly how you envisioned it months ago, and it came to pass the way you thought it would."

"There is power in seeing things as they can become, Mai Tee. When you do that, things will start to become what you think," Sani explained wisely.

"You are a man of great faith and foresight."

"Faith maybe, but foresight is hard to claim, because nobody knows what tomorrow brings," Sani said with a smile covering his entire face.

The couple began to discuss how each of Sani's warriors tried to refuse the beast they had been offered by Sani. Sani could not keep everything, not with the help he received from his loyal friends. Eventually they agreed and happily left with their families to celebrate too. Sani encouraged them to come to him whenever they needed anything; the waterhole had become a source of income for Sani and all his associates.

CHAPTER EIGHT

LET OTHERS JOIN THE HUNTING

The news about Sani's success had crossed the borders of Zimuto and most of the village gossips that crossed paths with members of Sani's family expressed great depths of embarrassment for their words and actions prior to the new discovery. Now most of their families needed to go to Sani's house instead of the hunting grounds for their next meal. This showed how fast life's status ranking can change: one moment you are on top of the world and another you're down, or vice versa. Sani had instructed his family to be very fair and kind to everyone who visibly showed acts of unkindness to them during their difficult time.

"Listen, my children, no member of my family will seek re-venge for what some villagers did or said about us. The past is gone, and I urge you to keep your focus on the future, do you hear me?"

"Yes Baba," they all responded.

"No need to spend your most valued energy towards the past when you know your next life is in the future. What you do today must correct the past and create future opportunities, understood?"

"Yes Baba," his children answered.

"I want you to invite all such people to the feast this week-end." Sani paused then continued. "I want all of you to hear me tell this to Tee. Son, I am proud of our accomplishments at the waterhole, but I am more so proud of you. Now you can start your preparations to go to school in the city."

"Thank you, Baba." Tee's eyes were filling with tears by the time he looked up to acknowledge his dad.

The day of the feast...

The long-planned day of celebration had arrived. As ex-pected, the chief and his delegation arrived early for private discussions with Sani. Sani had indicated to him weeks before that he wanted to bring relevance into the village of Zimuto. He wanted to show that one person, when helped by many, can make a great impact in the community. From the beginning Sani did not see wealth as the goal; he consistently addressed it as a means to a goal. His goal was to put his family in a position where it would never need to worry about essentials and to bring the same to other the families in Zimuto. He had shared his goal with his best friend, the Chief of Zimuto.

"How did you pay for this big feast?" Chief Gato asked.

"Each time I need anything, I go to the waterhole to get a beast. That is my source of income," Sani explained.

"You know, my friend, this waterhole has really become a pride of the village. Everyone is talking about how they no longer have to risk their lives in the hunting grounds for a beast to share." The chief explained the impact of Sani's creation to the entire community.

"I am honored, Chief It has been the dream of my son and I that things would come out that way," Sani acknowledged the chief's compliment.

"Everything is easy for you, my friend," the chief said.

"Chief, I assure you that nothing great comes without sleepless nights, thoughts of doubt and conflict. All that we experienced in the course of this achievement involved overcoming adversity," Sani explained.

"I understand, Sani...."

Sani interrupted the Chief and whistled out for Tee. "I have something for you, chief."

"Sani, an award is given to the victor; you should be getting one."

"I will accept no award for working hard for my family; every man should do so. I will accept no award for helping my own people; every villager should do the same," Sani said in an emotional voice.

Tee appeared carrying two polished antelope horns that had been carved to show a picture of a great warrior, the chief's late father. Sani directed Tee to give them to Chief. The horns had also been engraved with words which translated to, "Everything you honor, will come towards you."

The chief expressed his gratitude for the well-thought-out gift.

"I wish I knew how to repay you for this moment, Sani."

"Your heart speaks for itself, Chief; I know you care more than you tell."

Soon the banquet began and hundreds of guests were jubilating and ululating around Sani's compound. Some brought gifts despite Sani expressly forbidding any such act. As customary, many villagers couldn't travel distant journeys to return home during the night, and as such, the feast lasted all night in the village. That night, Sani announced the plan about the butchery to all the villagers present and everyone was very grateful and excited.

Running the butchery...

Construction at the butchery was at an advanced stage under the supervision of the twins. Sani and Tee had been attending the government business training program. They were taught hygiene, and how to cut beasts in a less wasteful manner. Training was complete in just a few weeks and the butchery was open for business. The government worker was surprised by the fact that the butchery was always well stocked with meats from all types of animals, such as antelope, deer, cattle, goat, chicken and fish.

As the months went by, Sani and Tee worked more and more each day. They had to go hunting at the waterhole, bring the meat in to the butchery and man the shop during the day. It almost seemed as if wealth had come at the cost of time and effort; to make matters worse, Sani had a partially functional left arm. One night during his routine of complaining to his wife about his hectic day, an idea came about,

"Baba Tee, you have a lot of people that love to help. Why don't you get some of them to do some of these hectic duties?" Mai Tee asked her husband.

"I don't think they can do a good job."

"Do you think you can do all the jobs by yourself better than each would do a portion of each job?" She persisted along her line of argument.

"I guess I have to think about it," Sani responded.

The next morning Sani woke up in a pleasant mood. He called out for his wife.

"Mai Tee, I have an idea, I have decided to get hunters to do the hunting, and more people to help at the butchery. I would compensate each with a beast every week. What do you think of my idea?" he asked his wife.

"Very well thought out, Baba Tee," she encouraged her husband.

"I have already sent Tee to tell the people. Since he is about to leave for the city, I should have these people help me," Sani continued.

"Well said," Mai Tee remarked as she left Sani standing in his excitement.

Sani could not understand why his wife, who habitually encouraged him, was acting as if he had stolen something from her. Anyway, work needed to be done, so he set off towards the butchery. Tee soon arrived with nine men; all of them were experienced hunters. Sani gave them instructions on taking turns to hunt in threes, only on his order. The men thought the offer of a beast per week was more than generous, so they graciously accepted. Now Sani needed four people to help in the butchery. A few hours later Tee walked in with three men; one of the two younger men looked familiar.

"Who are you, young man?" Sani asked.

"You forgot him, Baba?" Tee interjected.

"Refresh my memory, please."

"The fight a month ago..."

"Oh, yes. I thought your face looked familiar," Sani said as he extended his hand towards Jona for a handshake.

The elderly man was Mr. Hove, who Sani was delighted to see and grateful that he would accept such an offer. The presence of the hunters and the helpers at the butchery made Sani's work bearable. As the government workers throughout the community continued to teach people how to use the national currency instead of barter options, more and more people came to the butchery. The increase in the number of people seeking meat, instead of beasts, forced Sani to hire two more people, but this time they were both women. Cleanliness could never be achieved in a place where men worked alone, so the presence of ladies changed everything at the butchery.

After some weeks Tee left to go to university in the city; Sani missed him immensely, so he began spending less and less time doing chores at the butchery. Mr. Hove was now looking after the main activities of the butchery and Jona was a hard worker who complemented him well.

Soon after, Sani offered both Mr. Hove and Jona two beasts a week for their efforts. He also told the hunters that they would now be paid half a beast each time they hunted instead of a beast every week. The hunters loved this option because it meant more beasts in a week if they hunted more times, if you can call it hunting at the waterhole, anyway. So they began circling the village spreading the news about the butchery. Soon the news spread to other villages and of course - the more people came to the butchery, the more hunting was required, and the more satisfied everyone went home.

The culture of Zimuto had changed in one summer, and Sani was in the middle of it all. He became a much-respected man in Zimuto, not for his riches, but more for what he used his riches for. He was now an idol to most chiefs in the region. To Sani, life was for a cause and the money was a means for enabling the cause. He was thankful for the opportunity, the provision, the peace and the happiness.

CHAPTER NINE

SHARE IT WITH OTHER VILLAGES

About a month after Tee had left to attend university in the city, Sani received a delegation of royal visitors. The men, dressed in black and brown gowns, approached his homestead in a convoy of carts. Several warriors were visible in each cart, and that sparked Sani's protective instinct. A visibly frantic Sani jumped and called for his wife to run behind the compound with his daughters as he fetched his spear. Mai Tee obeyed without question and in a few seconds she had the girls out of sight. Sani took position behind a tree closest to his compound gateway.

"Who comes in surprise?" Sani asked.

The delegation tried to follow the direction of the voice to get to a human being but they could not find anybody in sight.

"We come in peace and we are looking for Sani of Zimuto."

"Who are you and why do you want Sani?" Sani continued his line of questioning.

One man of large build stood up in a cart near the front. He had a shaggy beard and tangled hair. His headgear proved that he was a chief.

"Sani, is that you?" The man spoke with authority. "I am Chief Muto of Zaka and have come in peace with my friends from surrounding villages."

Sani knew who Chief Muto was; he had met him before. However, this man had an oversized belly and weighed a lot more than the chief he remembered. Nevertheless, Sani came out to greet the delegation.

"My apologies, Chief, you look different." Sani spoke after finally recognizing the chief.

"We are here because we got the message you sent with the government workers," the chief said. "We truly need your help and thought we should come to you instead of having you come to our respective villages."

"I am honored, gentlemen. Please, come in; we can talk in more detail." Sani's face lightened up as he directed the men into the compound.

Three weeks before that day, Sani had instructed all government workers to tell chiefs in nearby villages about his willingness to help develop a waterhole system in their villages.

Unknown to him, Chief Muto had met with nine other chiefs to personally come and ask for Sani's help to develop the waterhole system in their villages. Sani was more than glad to help, as he showed them the skins from slaughtered beasts he was sending to the city upon Tee's request. He bragged that Tee had told him that the skins could fetch a thousand currencies each.

"Gentlemen, this is the least I can do. The government taught me a lot, and I no longer engage in barter trade with the beasts. I now slaughter them and sell the meat for 10 currencies per weight. I will show you how to open current accounts in the Mobile Bank and how to deposit all proceeds from the sale of the meat in the butchery. I will train each of your chosen people in everything. Tee also wrote some of the activities down, and I am more than willing to share them with you if you have someone who can read."

"We all can read," the chiefs responded with pride. "We learned from the school masters."

"Very well then, you are better than I was when I started," Sani said.

Chief Zaka spoke on behalf of all the delegation. "We hear what you will do for us, but what can we do for you in return? As you know, our ancestors say, one full plate returns with another."

Sani paused for a moment and said, "I want one hundred currencies for every beast slaughtered from each village every month deposited in the Mobile Bank, Additionally, I also want ten thousand currencies upfront for building each butchery."

"It is more generous than we thought, Sani. We accept your request." Chief Zaka spoke boldly as the other chiefs nodded in agreement.

Two weeks after the meeting, Sani began work in Zaka Village and then went to Charu Village, followed by Mbira Village, until all ten villages had the waterhole system set up and running swiftly. At first Sani did not notice much difference until one day when the Mobile Banker came to his compound.

"Sani, did you know that I just banked currency equivalent to a thousand beasts from the ten villages you helped last month?" the Banker informed Sani.

Sani smiled and asked, "How much in total did you collect this month?"

"One hundred thousand", the Banker responded, "and it will increase as the months go by, according to Chief Zaka."

Sani was filled with excitement. As a result, he decided to visit Chief Gato, his longtime friend, the following morning.

"My friend, I have a proposition for you." Sani conversed intimately with the chief.

"Speak. Let me hear your words, Sani," the chief eagerly responded.

"I want to hand over the use of the waterhole to the village of Zimuto. That means you become responsible for its function. I will train whoever you choose and be available when I am needed."

"Wait, wait, wait!" The Chief interrupted Sani. "I know you are excited about your success, Sani, but don't bet the field be-

THE WATERHOLE MILLIONAIRE

fore the rains come."

Sani chuckled before he spoke. "Who said I am doing it for free?"

"So how will you benefit from giving away your entire source of wealth?" the Chief boldly proclaimed.

"Gato, I have thought about it and as you already know, my proposition is working in ten other villages," Sani stated.

The chief knew whenever Sani addressed him with his last name, he was serious.

"How can we ever repay you for such a gift?" Chief spoke.

"It's not a gift. Here is what you will do for me, Chief. I want you to introduce me to ten other chiefs who need help with my work," Sani requested.

"Are you drunk, Sani? I can do that without you giving away your wealth."

"No, Chief, I am not finished. Then I want you to pay me one hundred currencies for every beast slaughtered from the waterhole each month until I tell you to stop." Sani finally finished his request.

"I see…. So this works well for you?" Chief asked.

"Yes, because I am getting one hundred thousand currencies from ten villages every month. If you give me ten more villages paying me another one hundred thousand each month, I will give you whatever I receive from Mvuu waterhole to use in your own household and in the Zimuto Village."

"God has made you a clever and generous man, Sani. I see what you mean and it makes a lot of sense. As of now, this day,

83

I promise you that it is done." Chief made a vow by shaking hands with Sani.

Three months from that day, the events happened exactly as planned by Sani. Zimuto had another reason to throw a feast of thanksgiving. This time the host was Chief Gato. God had blessed Sani again. He no longer had to wake up early to supervise his waterhole activities. He now spent time visiting Tee in the city with his wife and daughters. He was now learning about city businesses and wealth from his son. What a journey this modest man of Zimuto travelled in a short space of time.

CHAPTER TEN

ENJOY FRUITS OF THE
HARVEST...

It had been fourteen years since the life-changing summer
in the land of Zimuto. Sani had built a legacy from his ability to change lives, village after village. After graduating with
a degree in Economics, Tee had gone back to Zimuto to marry
Chipo, whom he had secretly admired since his first year as a
teenager.

Due to Tee's exceptional academic record, the university
had invited him to return and pursue a Master of Science in
Economics and Entrepreneurship degree, sponsored by the
International Finance Corporation (IFC). The IFC is a mem-

ber organization of the World Bank, and at the time, was the largest global development institution focused on the private sector in developing countries.

Upon his second graduation, Tee took a job with the IFC helping entrepreneurs and growing companies in member countries of the Southern Africa Development Community (SADC). Tee often told his parents that he had seen it all when it came to business and while each business was different, the principles for building and making each one a success were the same, and he credited his quick business wit to the lessons that he learned from his father. After three years with the IFC, Tee started the Zimuto Fund, which his father agreed to capitalize using money from his waterhole ventures that had by then multiplied to a hundred villages in the entire country.

The Zimuto Fund was created to identify entrepreneurial business ventures that had a direct social and environmental impact on the targeted communities. Tee and his team worked hard to ensure that entrepreneurs leading the identified ventures understood the mission of the Zimuto Fund.

"I want you to understand what we are all about," Tee explained during an investment workshop for prospective business people. "Zimuto Fund has a threefold goal: people, planet and profit."

Tee continued, "We are looking for entrepreneurs that will change people's lives for the better, and protect the environment while making money. This is not a handout, nor a non-profit fund; we must make money in order to maximize our impact across the country and around the world."

In a few years Tee and his team had helped entrepreneurs to build dams, construct roads and set up schools in all the villages that his father had built the waterhole system in. Each project had an immensely positive impact on the target communities, each preserving the environment and generating a positive return on investment, both for the entrepreneur and the Fund.

One afternoon, Sani and Mai Tee were seated across the aisle from Tee and Chipo inside a Boeing 747-400 as it approached the JFK Airport in New York. His wife was sitting in seat 7A by the window as the big jet hovered past clouds on its approach towards Runway 3 at JFK airport.

"What made you who you are, Tee?" Chipo spoke as she turned to face Tee.

"What do you mean?"

"The wisdom, the courage, and the strength – how did you develop all that by yourself?"

"Others pay thousands of currencies for the services of a wise counselor, but I had one as a father and another as a mother. Every single thing that I know today I learned from that man and that woman," Tee said pointing at his parents. "As part of my daily goal, I make learning something new a daily chore. I guess you can say that I've developed a habit for learning some-thing new every day."

Before Tee spoke again, a male voice came through the intercom. "Ladies and gentlemen, we have been cleared to land; please fasten your seat belts, make sure you are comfortably seated and that all electronics have been turned off."

"Why do you ask me that question now after all these years?" Tee quizzed his wife.

"I was just thinking about how you managed to get invited as a keynote speaker at the World Impact Forum in New York." She paused before continuing, "Everyone at the hospital has been envying me. They keep telling me to resign as a nurse and become your secretary."

"Well, are you?"

"Am I what?"

"Are you going to resign and take a job at the Zimuto Fund?" Tee clarified.

"Not a chance."

"Why not?"

"Let's just say I prefer you as a husband and not as a boss," she said, smiling at Tee.

They both laughed, and twenty minutes later the plane touched down. Tee had been invited to speak on how his father changed millions of lives while living in rural Zimuto, and how Tee used that experience to build an empire at the Zimuto Fund. Apparently this was a topic that Tee had spoken on at many events over the past few years. At the request of the

World Impact Forum Committee, Tee had brought along his father, who was due to receive a surprise Global Impact Award. Sani was obviously unaware of the award; in his mind he was accompanying his son to accept a very special global award before a group of a thousand entrepreneurs and community leaders.

Getting the award...

On the day of Tee's much-anticipated lecture, Sani's family arrived early and met up with Molly César. Molly was a Harvard Business School alumnus who was the secretary of the World Impact Forum Committee. She was assigned to host Tee and his family. The group entered the Griswold Coliseum, adjacent to Times Square, and by far the most decorated building in midtown Manhattan. The coliseum was filled with a crowd of five thousand people. At that time nobody noticed the family's arrival, as the event still had another sixty minutes before proceedings commenced. Tee and his family took their seats in the front row nearest to the stage. Everyone was eagerly anticipating the presentation from the managing director of the Zimuto Fund, Africa's most prosperous impact investing business model. They all wanted to know how Tee learned the principles they had heard are fundamental to the making of any successful impact business. It was not long before Jim Fish took the podium to open the event.

"Ladies and gentlemen, welcome to the first day of the

World Impact Forum. I am honored to stand before some of the greatest business minds this century has seen. This year we have a special guest, or guests to be more accurate, as you will see in a moment. Before we get into the opening presentation, I want to invite Mr. Chairman to come up and present the Impact Award to a man who most of you have not seen or heard of before. The reason why is due to where he comes from. This man lived in a village in the southern part of Zimbabwe.

"A warrior by profession, he and his family made a living hunting and exchanging wild meat for other complementing commodities. This man encountered a life-changing event that would have sent many people to their lifelong days of misery; that event revealed his destiny. Ladies and gentlemen, more words would tarnish the real essence of this man's accomplishments. A deca-millionaire in our currency terms, he built his empire by creating a business system that enriched people around him first, before enriching himself. News about this man's great success got to us through the local IFC office that had worked with his son. This man applied the same principles in building Africa's most successful impact fund and we could not resist the temptation to award him this year's Impact Award for the entrepreneur whose efforts created maximum impact in his community. Without further ado, let me present the Impact Award winner, Sani of Zimuto!"

The coliseum burst into applause as Sani looked around in shock.

"I thought this was your day," he said as he gazed at his son.

Then, he stood and began to cautiously walk towards the podium.

Sani shook Mr. Chairman's hand and was presented with a gold-plated shield with the words "Business Impact Award" and his name engraved below it. Jim handed Sani a microphone and asked him to say a few words. He paused for a few seconds as the coliseum applause subsided, looking extremely surprised and visibly out of words to express his emotions. Sani looked up at the capacity crowd and began talking slowly.

"There is no greater form of happiness for a father than that experienced when his son and friends honor him." Sani spoke with his voice rasping as he approached the brink of a teary phase. "I came here as a guest and became the hero before the event even started. Thank you all for such heartfelt love and for this piece of honor that I will cherish until my death. I could not predict this event ten years ago, but I could see the future of my life and I desperately wanted to be there."

The crowd responded in resounding applause while standing to their feet. Sani waited for them to take their seats before proceeding. "No man can willingly go to a place he has not first seen in his mind. As a result, I had to see a future better than the one I was living at the time. What I saw was a better Zimuto, a better family and ultimately a better me, and so I began travelling that journey. So I want to thank all of you for making me feel that I have reached my destination."

The crowd rose again, this time with deafening applause. Sani's emotions could not let him continue, so he handed the microphone back to Jim. He wiped his teary eyes and began waving at the audience as he made his way back to his seat.

After about a minute, the audience finally sat down and Jim paused while trying to compose himself. Eventually he did and began talking.

"I promise you that we did not plan for this moment to be this emotional. Powerful moments cannot be stopped. Without wasting time, let me get into the subject of the next man from Zimuto. He is a proven business leader who went through the most intensive entrepreneurship training by working with his father, Sani. His ability to learn and attach the principles his father taught him to modern-day business impressed our committee; as a result, we could not resist his insight, wisdom and great experience to deliver the World Impact Forum Keynote presentation. Ladies and gentlemen, help me welcome this year's keynote speaker, Mr. Tindo of Zimuto."

The audience rose from their seats while clapping as Tee made his way to the podium. Tee was dressed in a dark blue suit gifted to him by his wife. His red tie complemented the light blue shirt and dark suit. He wore short hair and was six feet tall. A handsome man by any manner of judgment; Tee smiled more than he frowned, and laughed more that he sulked in his life. His parents and wife sat quietly, pleased to see him on the podium. His father had never before heard Tee give a presentation on the ten lessons he learned from his father that changed his business life. So he listened attentively as Tee arranged his presentation notes in to sequential order.

Tee began speaking,

"Thank you for this precious moment. It is an overwhelming experience for me to stand in front of businessmen and women I have read about as movers of industry and ambassadors of real-life impact. My lecture today is personal, although I have broken it down into ten simple lessons. For those of you intending to get into business, or those eager to create lifelong changes in your communities; it is not the end but rather the beginning of a new perspective on building business with a grander purpose.

You may ask, why business, why not other vehicles of income? I believe that life revolves around business. Look at the person next to you, what are they wearing? What are they sitting on? What are they writing with? Think back to where you live, the house, the car, the food, the utensils and the furniture. They all came about because of business. People just like you and me developed an idea, monetized it and began to generate cash flow. It is therefore correct to conclude that life revolves around business. I have yet to see a better cash-flow vehicle that can generate a lot of money on a continuous basis than a business venture. As a result, it makes sense if you have a heart for improving people's lives, to use a business as a vehicle for creating that kind of change.

I know there are many fears about business ventures, mainly because people witness a lot of them fail and a lot of lives being hurt as a result. I want you to know that 80 percent of business problems are caused by people, and the other 20 percent by other people. Therefore, business is about people, the people that run the enterprise and the people that benefit from the business. Business is also about learning from others; I have learned more in a business setup than I did in a school setup. I learned from watching my father, his village men and by reading how other great men and women changed the lives of people around them. I feel strongly about the need to change other people's lives. I also feel strongly about using the most powerful tool to do so, a business venture.

There are many lessons I learned from my father throughout my life. I learned how to overcome adversity, how to serve others and how to run a business. Today I will focus on the lessons I feel contributed to me understanding how to maximize positive impact on others. There are ten lessons I learned. If you grasp them, I truly believe they will give you the ability to turn ideas into cash flow, and ultimately, into social impact.

I will never forget the day my father told me that everything comes from somewhere, so you will need someone to help take it from somewhere and bring into your life. My father was that someone in my life. He helped bring the vision of Zimuto Fund into my life. It happened by learning and allowing myself to be his protégé."

Tee continued his presentation for the following hour, engaging the capacity audience and revealing the principles necessary for anybody to become a *Waterhole Millionaire*.

Are you a *Waterhole Millionaire*?

S. GABRIEL SHUMBA

Where you are, today is a result of what you have done with opportunities that came your way...
—S. Gabriel Shumba.

THE WATERHOLE
MILLIONAIRE

Waterhole Definitions

drought
/drout/
a pervasive problem

gra·zer
/ˈgrāzər/
a reward for overcoming a pervasive problem

hunt·ing
/ˈhən(t)iNG/
the process of solving a pervasive problem

hunt·ing ground
/ˈhən(t)iNG/ /ˈground/
a place where a reward is received

li·on
/ˈlīən/
a challenge standing in the way of a solution

mil.lion.aire
/milyəˈner,ˈmilyəˌner/
a person who is financially independent at any income level

son
/ˈsən/
a committed protégé

vil·lage
/ˈvilij/
a community of people in need

war·ri.or
/ˈwôrēər/
a dream driven person

wa·ter·hole
/ˈwôdərˌhōl,ˈwädərˌhōl/
a life changing solution to a pervasive problem

MISSION
WATERHOLE

I am on a mission to transform one million lives from the jaws of poverty in Africa in to the liberty of financial independence. As a result, I am looking for mission partners, so I implore you to find out more about my initiatives by going to:

www.missionwaterhole.com/initiatives

FOR SPECIAL ORDERS

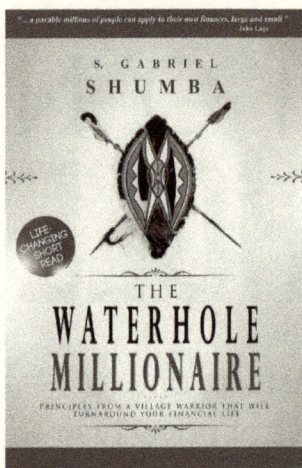

Special orders of the book, *The Waterhole Millionaire* are available at quantity discounts for bulk purchases, school curriculum, fund-raising or church training and business workshops.

Study books and leadership workbooks are available for business training, school curriculum and other training uses.

Contact, Munaii Bookworks, for complete details or bulk quantity purchases.

To order individual copies of the book go to:

http://www.Waterholemillionaire.com

The Waterhole Millionaire

ISBN 978-0-9861018-1-6

ABOUT THE AUTHOR

S. Gabriel Shumba is an entrepreneur, venture investor and a strong advocate for impact-driven businesses. He is an inspirational leader who speaks on various corporate, community and economic platforms on the subjects of frontier investing and collective impact to bring about personal financial independence. He volunteers on many levels and is passionate about developing African communities, inspiring transformational leadership, developing ventures, and alternative solutions to poverty. Gabriel is the Founder of Group Shumba, a private equity and investment advisory firm, and Founder of Mission Waterhole, the organization that pursues his mission of improving lives of people facing financial hardship. He sits on many corporate and community boards and mentors students, professionals and entrepreneurs around the world. He believes in the power that entrepreneurship has in changing the lives of people, especially in frontier geographies.

www.ingramcontent.com/pod-product-compliance
Lightning Source LLC
Chambersburg PA
CBHW021821090426
42811CB00032B/1971/J